I Know the Scriptures Are True: Sharing Time Ideas 1998

By
Susan Luke

Covenant Communications, Inc.

In loving memory of my grandmother, Blanche Privat.

Acknowledgments

Pages 8 and 43 reproduced using The Print Shop Deluxe Companion,
Copyright © 1994, Broderbund Software, Inc. & ImageBuilder Software, Inc.

Page 70 and various fonts throughout the book reproduced using
The Print Shop Deluxe, Copyright © 1993-1994, Broderbund Software, Inc.

Copyright © 1997 by Susan Luke
All rights reserved. Permission is hereby granted
with purchase to reproduce any part of this book
on a limited basis for personal and class use only.
Reproduction of any part of this book for
commercial use is expressly prohibited.

Printed in the United States of America
First Printing: October 1998
97 98 99 00 01 02   10 9 8 7 6 5 4 3 2 1

I Know the Scriptures Are True: Sharing Time Ideas 1998
Cover Design by Val Bagley
Covenant Communications, Inc.
ISBN 1-57734-188-0

Table of Contents

The Scriptures Are the Word of God Revealed to Prophets 1

As I Study and Pray, I Will Come to Know and Love
the Scriptures and Feel the Influence of the Holy Ghost 4

The Scriptures Teach Me about the Life of Jesus Christ 15

The Scriptures Teach Me That Jesus Christ Provided the
Way for Me to Return to Heavenly Father 24

I Can Be Part of the Multitude to Whom the Lord or His
Prophet is Speaking in the Scriptures. 31

I Can Be like the Men and Women of God in the Scriptures 38

The Scriptures Give Me Courage to Live Righteously—
to Hold to the Iron Rod 44

The Scriptures Help Me Understand the Importance of
Making and Keeping Covenants 55

The Scriptures Teach Me That Heavenly Father Hears My Prayers 62

The Scriptures Teach Me That I Can Feel Joy When I
Share the Gospel Message 68

The Scriptures Help Me Feel Gratitude to Heavenly Father 73

The Scriptures Teach Me to Have Faith in Jesus Christ
and Live as He Lived 78

Introduction

What an exciting year this will be in Primary—to help children grow in their love for the scriptures! Throughout the year, children will learn more fully how to use the scriptures to find answers to questions, to learn gospel principles taught in the various stories, and to truly discover that the scriptures are the word of God and were written for our "profit and learning" (1 Nephi 19:23). The best time to learn a good habit is in the early years of life. Let's take advantage of the opportunity given us this year and help these children create a firm foundation of scripture study that will stay with them throughout their lives.

As I have said in previous sharing time books, the following lessons and ideas are merely a suggestion. Prayerfully consider each sharing time opportunity and let the Holy Spirit guide you as you determine the needs of your Primary. May the Lord bless you with all that is needed to teach the gospel to his little ones.

1. The Scriptures Are the Word of God Revealed to Prophets.

Preparation:

1. Copy onto card stock the reading chart found on page 3—one for each child.
2. Gather crayons or felt pens, and a sheet of small stickers for each child.
3. Invite bishopric-approved ward members to share their testimonies of the truthfulness of the scriptures.

Lesson:

Introduce the theme for the year by first singing, "Search, Ponder, and Pray" (*Children's Songbook*, p. 109), followed by a few ward members sharing their testimonies of the scriptures. Have the children locate and read aloud John 5:39. Bear your testimonies of the truthfulness of the scriptures and how by searching them, you will find Christ. Hand out the reading charts, and if time permits, let the children color them. Give each of the children a sheet of stickers, and encourage them to place a sticker on their chart for each day they read their scriptures.

Additional Ideas:

- Display various books containing histories, poems, warnings, instructions, stories, etc. Briefly discuss each book and the importance of the words contained in each. Explain that we can find the same kinds of things (history, poems, etc.) in the scriptures. Ask the children what the difference is between the scriptures and the other books displayed. The scriptures are the word of God revealed to prophets. We can read about our forefathers in history books, and the information may be true, but it is not scripture because it was not revealed to and written down by a prophet of God. To understand more fully how this form of revelation works, view a portion of the Church video, "Restoration of the Priesthood." Prior to sharing time, advance the video to the part when Joseph Smith receives revelation and writes it down as scripture. If the video is not available, invite some priesthood holders to role-play a situation where a prophet receives scripture through revelation.

- Gather as many of the following objects as possible, with each object representing a story from the scriptures:

toy ship	Nephi
slingshot	David & Goliath
multi-colored cloth	Joseph's coat
small white stones	Brother of Jared
small iron rod	Lehi's dream
plastic animals	Noah
stuffed lion	Daniel
fruit	Word of Wisdom
compass	Liahona
torn piece of cloth	Title of Liberty
pioneer bonnet	Pioneer stories
toy whale	Jonah
missionary tag	Ammon
dime	Tithing
salt	Lot's wife
toy sword	Anti-Nephi-Lehies

    Place the objects on a table and cover them with a cloth. Give each child a piece of paper and a pencil. Have the children come forward, remove the cloth, and let them study the objects for 15-30 seconds. Cover the objects again with the cloth and ask the children to sit down. At your signal, ask the children to write down as many of the objects as they can remember. Tell them not worry if they don't remember all of them. After a couple of minutes, have them stop, put their pencils down, and listen as you tell a little bit about each object. One by one, briefly tell the scripture story represented by each object. When finished, ask if any of the children were able to remember and write down all the items. Most likely, you will not have any child who remembers them all. This activity demonstrates the importance of writing down scripture. Heavenly Father has revealed to his prophets his words and counsel concerning us. If ancient and modern-day prophets neglected to write down the words of God, we would not have many of the stories and instructions found in the scriptures. Many people would dwindle in unbelief and fall away from the commandments of the Lord.

- In order for a prophet to receive revelation and write it down as scripture, he must be in tune with the Spirit of the Lord. To demonstrate this, invite 2-3 children to come forward. Blindfold each child and give them a piece of chalk. Recite a simple scripture and ask the children to write the words on the chalkboard, even though they are unable to see the words they are writing. Chances are, when finished, their writing will be hard to read. Liken the blindfolds to spiritual darkness, which occurs when the commandments of the Lord are disobeyed or ignored. When a prophet is not in tune, he is unable to clearly receive revelation from Heavenly Father. Perform the experiment again with the blindfolds removed. With the spiritual darkness removed, a prophet can be in tune with the Spirit, making revelation easier to receive and understand.

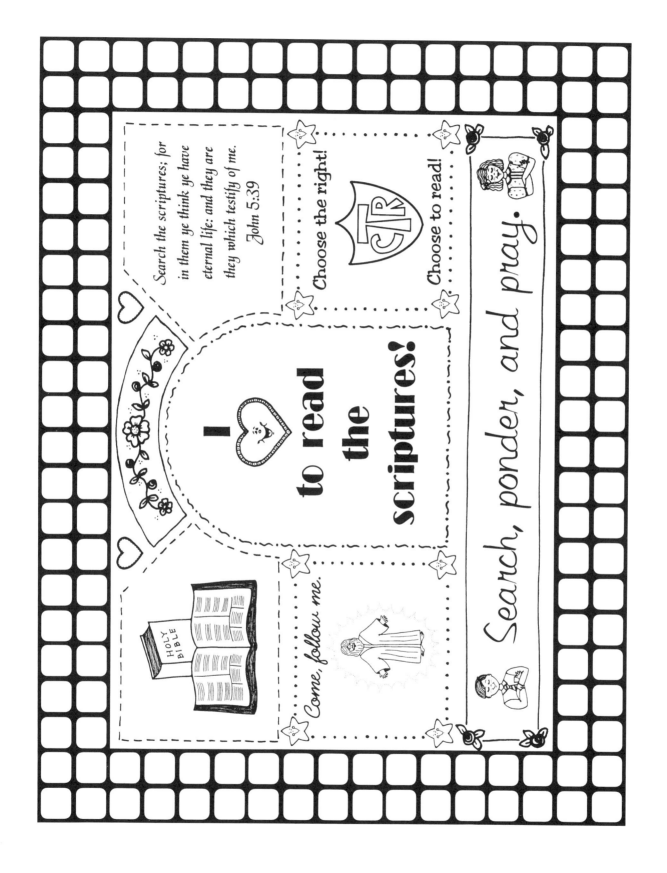

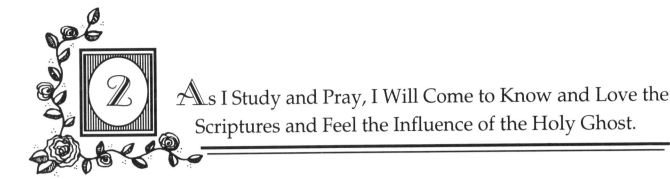

As I Study and Pray, I Will Come to Know and Love the Scriptures and Feel the Influence of the Holy Ghost.

Preparation:

1. Copy the worksheet on pages 6 and 7 front to back (one worksheet for each child).
2. Gather various tools for display: Hammer, ruler, measuring cup, scissors, needle and thread, etc.
3. Gather scriptures and, if possible, an LDS scripture marker for each child (available through Church distribution centers).

Lesson:

Display the various tools you have gathered and discuss with the children how each tool helps us to perform specific tasks. We have available to us other tools that help us to understand the scriptures. The Topical Guide, Bible Dictionary, footnotes, Joseph Smith Translation, maps, scripture markers, and prayer are some of the tools we use to help us when studying the scriptures. Explain each scripture tool, where it is located, and how it is used. Give each child a worksheet and a scripture marker or plain pencil. Divide the children into small groups and assign a Primary worker to each group to help the children as needed. If time permits, have the children share their answers. Encourage the children to take their worksheets home and share the information with their families. **Note:** Prior to presenting this sharing time, it may be useful to send a copy of the worksheet home with the Primary workers who will be helping. This will give them time to study and prepare for their part in helping the children.

Additional Ideas:

- The Sunday before you present the following sharing time, copy the reminder slips on page 8 and send one home with each child. Copy the bookmarks on page 9—one bookmark for each child. Gather pencils, crayons, and/or felt pens. During sharing time, invite the children to come forward one at a time and share with the Primary their favorite scripture and why. After each child has had a chance to share, hand out a bookmark for each child. Let them color the bookmarks and write the references to their favorite scriptures on the lines provided.

- Copy the heart on page 10—one for each child. Copy the scripture references on page 11 and cut apart. At the beginning of sharing time, hand the scripture references to several children. Explain that they are going to search their scriptures to learn about the Holy Ghost—his mission, his names, how his influence is felt, etc. Beginning with the first reference, have the child locate and read aloud the assigned scripture. Take a few minutes to elaborate and explain the scripture. Continue until all scripture references have been read. Help the children understand that as our lives are influenced by the Holy Ghost, our hearts are filled with love and peace. Give each child a heart and encourage the children to color in one line for every time they feel the influence of the Holy Ghost.

- Copy and cut out the footprints on pages 12 through 14. Gather a flashlight and label it "Holy Ghost." Prior to the start of sharing time, tape the footprints to the floor, creating a pathway leading to a picture of Christ. Using the reference of Psalm 119:105, Elder Boyd K. Packer once said, "The still, small voice of the Holy Ghost is a light unto [our] feet, and a lamp unto [our] path" (*Ensign*, November, 1989). Turn the room lights out and explain that the Holy Ghost is a great tool to us in understanding the scriptures. Without his influence, we can be left in the dark spiritually. By obedience to the commandments, we can be worthy of his influence. Shine the flashlight on the footsteps and read what is written as you walk along the path. Briefly discuss each scripture. With the help of the Holy Ghost, we can follow the path that leads to the Savior.

Additional Resources:

A game demonstrating the influence of the Holy Ghost can be found on page 14 of *Awesome Family Nights*. (© 1994 Susan Luke, Covenant Communications, Inc.)

LDS SCRIPTURE MARKER

1. What do the following abbreviations mean? (Hint: Look in the first few pages of the Bible or Book of Mormon.)

   TG _____   JST _____

   BD _____   HC _____

   JS-M _____   JS-H _____

   A of F _____   HEB _____

   GR _____   IE _____

2. Look up "Baptism" in the Topical Guide. List the first three scripture references given:

   1. _____
   2. _____
   3. _____

3. Are there any scripture references on "Baptism" in the Doctrine & Covenants?_____ Old Testament?_____ Book of Mormon?_____

4. In the Bible Dictionary, what is the Greek meaning of the word "Genesis"?_____

5. Look up and read Luke 4:5 in the New Testament, including the Joseph Smith Translation (JST) found in the footnotes. According to the JST, who takes Jesus to the high mountain—the devil or the Spirit? _____

6. If the JST is too long to be included in the footnotes, where would you locate it? (Hint: Look in the footnotes of Luke 3:13.)_____

7. Discuss with your group why you would use a scripture marker. Mark your favorite scripture or one that has special meaning to you.

8. Look up and read 3 Nephi 17:1-3. How can we use prayer as a tool to study the scriptures? _____

9. In 1 Nephi 15:11, what additional scripture references are given in the footnotes? List them.

   a. _____

   b. _____

   c. _____

10. What does the Gazetteer help us to understand? _____

11. Using the Gazetteer, what is the grid reference for Bethlehem on Map #1? _____ Can you locate Bethlehem on Map #1?

12. In the space below, write which tool you think will help you the most and why:

_____
_____
_____
_____
_____
_____
_____
_____
_____
_____
_____
_____
_____
_____
_____

Dear Family,

Would you please help me locate and mark my favorite scripture so that I might be prepared to share it next Sunday during Primary?

Thank you!

Dear Family,

Would you please help me locate and mark my favorite scripture so that I might be prepared to share it next Sunday during Primary?

Thank you!

Dear Family,

Would you please help me locate and mark my favorite scripture so that I might be prepared to share it next Sunday during Primary?

Thank you!

Dear Family,

Would you please help me locate and mark my favorite scripture so that I might be prepared to share it next Sunday during Primary?

Thank you!

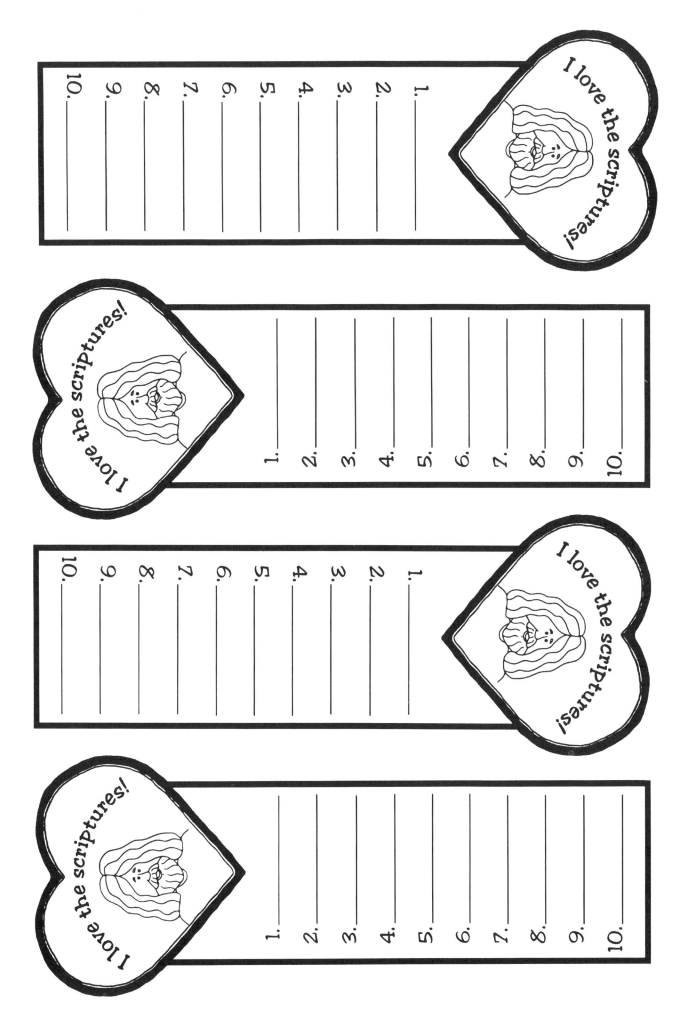

"Yea, behold, I will tell you in your mind and in your heart, by the Holy Ghost, which shall come upon you and which shall dwell in your heart." D&C 8:2

"And by the power of the Holy Ghost ye may know the truth of all things." Moroni 10:5

Color in one line every time you feel the influence of the Holy Ghost—whether it be while reading scriptures, saying a prayer, during testimony meeting, or at any other time in your life.

Luke 12:12	2 Nephi 32:5
John 14:26	Moroni 8:26
John 15:26	Moroni 10:5
Acts 5:32	D&C 35:6
1 Nephi 10:17	D&C 36:2
2 Nephi 31:12	D&C 76:116

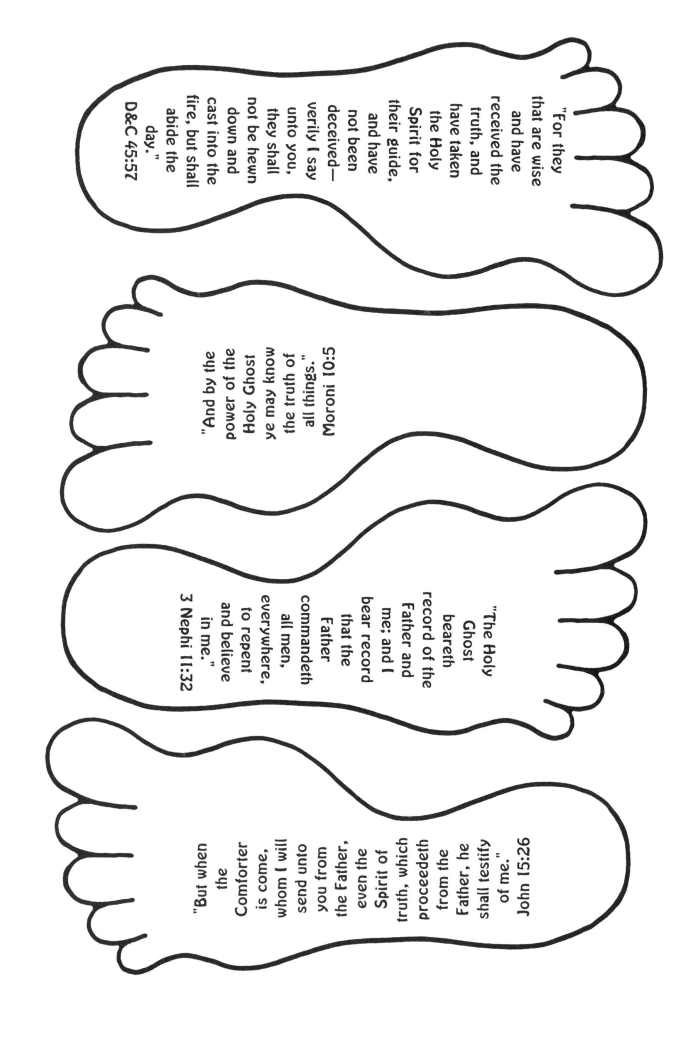

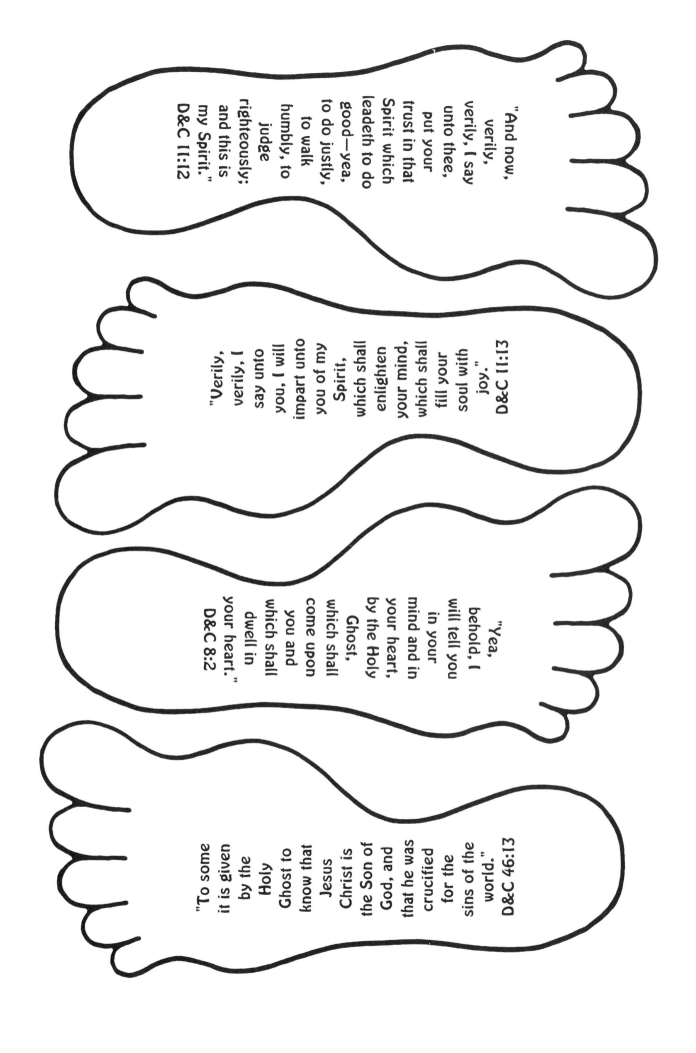

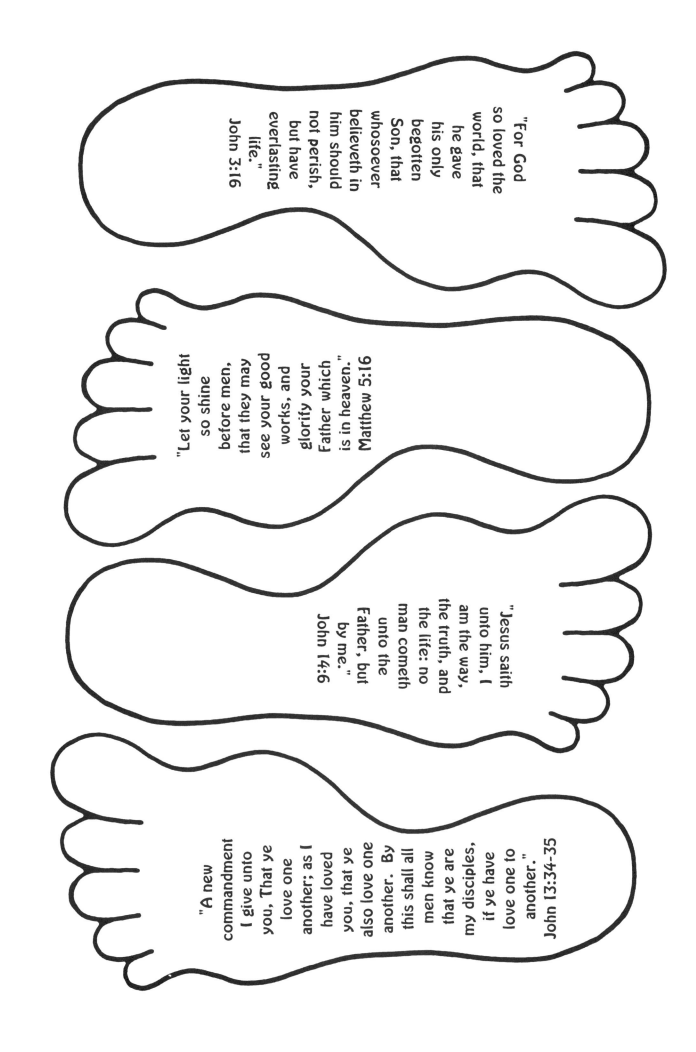

3. The Scriptures Teach Me about the Life of Jesus Christ.

Preparation:

1. Copy and cut out the fish found on pages 17 through 19. Place a paper clip on the mouth of each fish.
2. Gather a long stick, string, and magnet.
3. Make a fishing pole by tying the string to the end of the stick, then tying the magnet to the end of the string.

Lesson:

When Jesus began his ministry upon the earth, he called twelve disciples or apostles. Some of these men were fishermen by trade. In Matthew 4:18-22, Jesus invited these disciples to follow him so that he could make them "fishers of men." How did he make his disciples fishers of men? What did he teach them? What does Jesus want us to learn? Invite the children to come forward one at a time to "fish" for the answers to these and other questions. As each fish is caught, read the question first, then find the answer by referring to the scripture reference given. Discuss each principle that Jesus taught.

Additional Ideas:

- Gather four sacks and label them 1, 2, 3, and 4. Place in each sack various items that correlate with a story from Jesus' life. For example, a small basket, a piece of bread, and a toy fish could represent the story of Jesus feeding the 5,000. A toy ship and a clear jar (with a tight lid) filled with vinegar, oil, and blue food coloring could represent when Jesus calmed the tempest. (When the jar is tilted from end to end, waves are simulated.) Place the items in the sacks. Invite children to come forward one at a time and choose a sack. Let each child remove the items one at a time and try to guess the scripture story. When the story has been guessed, retell the story to the children.

- Invite four Primary workers ahead of time to each tell a story from the life of Jesus using pictures, puppets, flannel board figures, etc. Place each worker in a separate corner of the room. Divide the children into four groups and assign each group a different corner. Allow a few minutes for each Primary worker to relate their story, then have the groups switch to a new corner. Continue switching until each group has had the opportunity to hear each story.

- Copy and cut out the story segments found on pages 20 through 23. Gather a picture of the birth of Christ, twelve-year-old Jesus in the temple, Jesus' baptism, his crucifixion and resurrection. Place the pictures on a display board. Place the corresponding story segments out of order under each picture. Invite the children to come forward one at a time and place the story segments in the correct chronological order under each picture. After the story segments have been positioned correctly, briefly discuss each story with the children.

- Obtain a long roll of white paper. Gather crayons, pencils, and felt pens. Prior to sharing time, label in chronological order across the top (lengthwise) the various events in the life of Christ. Roll out the paper on the floor or across a couple of tables and let the children draw a mural depicting the life of Christ. Recount some of the stories as they draw. Display the mural in the Primary room when complete.

- Gather a dark overcoat, hat, and large magnifying glass. Prior to the start of sharing time, write scripture references that refer to the life of Christ on small slips of paper and hide them around the room. This will be your evidence. Role-play the part of a private detective, saying somthing like, "I heard that the scriptures teach about Jesus Christ. Well, I don't believe it. I want proof. I want evidence!" Slowly walk around the room with your magnifying glass, looking for evidence. When you find one of the slips of paper, shout, "Ah-ha! Evidence!" Have the children locate and read aloud the scripture reference. Briefly discuss the scripture, then look for another piece of evidence. Continue until all the "evidence" has been collected and there is proof of Jesus Christ in the scriptures. You may want to end by bearing your testimony of Jesus Christ. **Note:** This same private detective activity could be used with several of the coming months' themes. If you find it to be successful with your Primary, use it again to prove what each theme is claiming about the scriptures.

The Birth of Christ

Joseph and Mary traveled to Bethlehem to be taxed.

Jesus was born in a stable because there was no room in the inn.

Angels appeared to shepherds and told of the birth of the Savior.

The wise men followed the star to worship Jesus.

To escape King Herod, Joseph and Mary fled to Egypt.

Young Jesus in the Temple

Twelve-year-old Jesus and his parents traveled to Jerusalem for the feast of the Passover.

After traveling one day toward home, Joseph and Mary discovered Jesus was not among the group of family and friends.

Joseph and Mary returned to Jerusalem to search for Jesus.

After three days, Joseph and Mary found Jesus in the temple.

Jesus was teaching wise men and answering their questions.

The Baptism of Jesus

Jesus went with John the Baptist to the river Jordan.

John the Baptist questioned why he should baptize Jesus since Jesus had not sinned.

John the Baptist went down into the water and baptized Jesus.

Jesus came up straightway out of the water and the Spirit of God descended upon him.

A voice from heaven said, "This is my beloved Son, in whom I am well pleased. Hear ye him."

The Crucifixion of Christ

Jesus prepared the first sacrament for his Apostles during the last supper.

Jesus set an example for the Apostles by washing their feet.

Jesus suffered and prayed in the Garden of Gethsemane.

Jesus was betrayed by Judas Iscariot.

Jesus was taken to Calvary to be crucified on a cross.

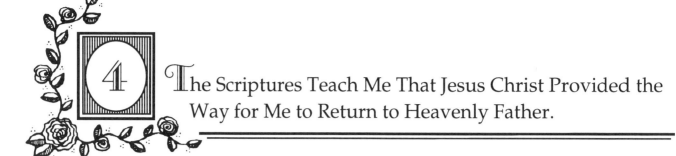

4. The Scriptures Teach Me That Jesus Christ Provided the Way for Me to Return to Heavenly Father.

Preparation:

1. Copy and cut out the visual aids found on pages 27 and 28.
2. Gather a chalkboard, chalk, eraser, and "Fun-tack."

Lesson:

Using "Fun-tack," place the picture of Heavenly Father in the center of the chalkboard surrounded closely by all the people. Use the chalk to draw a close circle around the group. Explain that in the premortal life, we all lived with our Heavenly Father. One by one, we were sent to earth through birth. (Move the people away from God and outside the circle.) The circle represents the veil that was placed between us and Heavenly Father. In other words, our memory of the premortal life was taken from us. Without this knowledge, how can we learn the steps needed to return to Heavenly Father? Jesus Christ has provided the way for us to return to Heavenly Father. We can find these steps in the scriptures. Each paper person has a scripture telling of a step we can take to help lead us back to Heavenly Father. Invite the children to come forward one at a time and choose a paper person. Read aloud the scripture given and discuss how it helps us return to Heavenly Father. Place the person close to Heavenly Father once again. Continue until all the people have returned to Heavenly Father.

Additional Ideas:

- Copy and cut out the questions and scripture references on pages 29 and 30. Gather various owner's manuals and instruction booklets for display. Explain to the children that when we play a new game, we learn it by referring to the instructions. Many bikes and toys need to be assembled after they are purchased. We refer to the owner's manual or instruction booklet for help. Briefly discuss some of the booklets you have brought for display. How hard would it be to assemble something or play a new game if we didn't have the instructions? The scriptures contain instructions from Heavenly Father on how we can return to live with him again. To demonstrate this, invite the children to come forward one at a time and choose a question. Find the answer to the question by locating and reading the scripture reference given for each. Continue until all questions have been answered. Encourage the children to search the scriptures to find answers to their questions.

• Play a form of "Simon Says," calling it "Jesus Says" instead. Move the Primary chairs out of the way and have the children line up at the back of the room. You stand at the head of the room. Read the statements found below—prompting all the children to move toward you by following the directions given. Each statement is something that Jesus taught. Explain to the children that as long as they do what Jesus says, they can move forward. If they do something contrary to the teachings of Jesus, such as push or shove someone, they will need to go back to the start. Continue until everyone reaches you. Encourage the children to always do as "Jesus Says" so they can return to Heavenly Father.

1. Jesus says to be baptized by immersion. (3 Nephi 11:22-27.) Hold your nose, crouch down, rise up, and move forward one step.

2. Jesus says to love one another. (John 13:34.) Give the person next to you a hug and move forward one step.

3. Jesus says to become like a little child—full of humility. (Matthew 18:3-4.) Take three baby steps forward.

4. Jesus says to serve one another. (Galatians 5:13.) Take someone by the hand and help them move forward one step.

5. Jesus says to pray always. (Luke 18:1.) Fold your arms, bow your head, and take one step forward.

6. Jesus says to trust in the Holy Ghost and he will lead you to do good. (D&C 11:12.) Move forward one step.

7. Jesus says to walk by faith, not by sight. (2 Corinthians 5:7.) Close your eyes and move forward one step.

8. Jesus says to forgive others. (Matthew 18:21-22.) Shake hands with the person next to you and take one step forward.

9. Jesus says if we obey the commandments of God we can enter into the kingdom of heaven. (Matthew 7:21.) Think of a way you can obey Heavenly Father. Raise your hand and share it with the rest of the Primary. After sharing, "enter into the kingdom of heaven" by moving the rest of the way to the front of the room.

- Play the part of the private detective as found in lesson three. Find evidence in the scriptures that Jesus Christ provided the way for us to return to Heavenly Father.

D&C 14:7	1 Nephi 13:37
3 Nephi 23:5	D&C 35:6
3 Nephi 9:22	2 Nephi 31:17
Acts 2:38	John 3:5
Mark 11:22-23	3 Nephi 27:16

 Do I need to be baptized in order to return to Heavenly Father?
Answer: John 3:5

 What do I need to do to be ready for baptism?
Answer: Acts 2:38

 What if I make a mistake? How do I become clean again?
Answer: Acts 22:16

 What promises do I make to the Lord at baptism?
Answer: Mosiah 18:10

 What should be my desire after baptism?
Answer: Mosiah 18:8-9

 Who will teach me and be my guide in this life?
Answer: John 14:26

 Who can I look to as an example to follow in this life?
Answer: 1 Peter 2:21

 What did Jesus do to make it possible for me to return to Heavenly Father?
Answer: 2 Nephi 2:6-8

5. I Can Be Part of the Multitude to Whom the Lord or His Prophet Is Speaking in the Scriptures.

Preparation:

1. Copy (and cut out for the younger children) the crown found on page 33—one for each child.
2. Gather scissors, crayons, and tape or stapler.
3. Invite someone to role play King Benjamin.

Lesson:

Invite a priesthood member from your ward or branch to role play King Benjamin giving his sermon found in Mosiah 1-6—condensing it, but covering the points of the sermon illustrated on the crown found on page 33. When finished, hand out the crowns. Allow the children time to draw pictures of King Benjamin's sermon in the spaces provided on the crown. Help the children cut out, and tape or staple their crowns together. Even though King Benjamin gave his sermon many years ago, the principles taught were of Jesus Christ and still apply to us today. Encourage the children to go home and teach King Benjamin's sermon to their families by following the pictures on the crown.

Additional Ideas:

- Copy and cut out the squares found on pages 34 through 37. Gather a beanbag and tape. Prior to the start of sharing time, tape the squares to the floor—four rows across and four rows down. Invite the children to take turns tossing the beanbag onto a square. When the beanbag lands on a square, read the square and have the child decide how that person, event, or commandment relates to them in their life today.

- Obtain a large piece of white paper, a felt pen, scratch paper, and pencils. Draw a large heart (approximately 25"-30" across) onto the paper, allowing room at the top to write the words of Deuteronomy 6:6. Attach the paper to a display board. Divide the children into small groups with a Primary worker assigned to help each group.

Give each group a piece of scratch paper, a pencil, and a couple of past conference issues of the *Ensign*. Explain: D&C 1:38 teaches us whether the Lord uses his own voice or the voice of his servants, the prophets, it is the same. We also learn from D&C 68:4 that when an elder of the Church speaks by the power of the Holy Ghost, it is scripture. Twice a year, the *Ensign* is filled with inspired words by the Lord's modern-day servants. When we listen to the conference talks, it is as if we are part of the multitudes that Christ spoke to when he was on the earth. His words are unchanging. The messages given in general conference are the same messages Christ gave; they are just presented in a way that we can understand for our time. Allow the groups about 5-7 minutes to skim through the stories and find "words of wisdom" that apply to them. Children can write their findings on their scratch paper. When the time is past, ask the groups to share their findings with the rest of the Primary. As they share, write the words inside the heart. Encourage the children to keep the words of the prophets in their hearts to lead them in righteousness.

• Obtain a chart of the Ten Commandments (65038) from your meetinghouse library. Display the chart for the children to see. Divide the children into five groups. If available, ask a Primary worker to help with each group. Give two commandments to each group and have children discuss what their assigned commandments mean and how they relate to their modern-day lives. When the group discussions are finished, have a member of each group share their information with the rest of the Primary. Explain that even though the ten commandments that Moses received were written long ago, we can still apply them in our lives today.

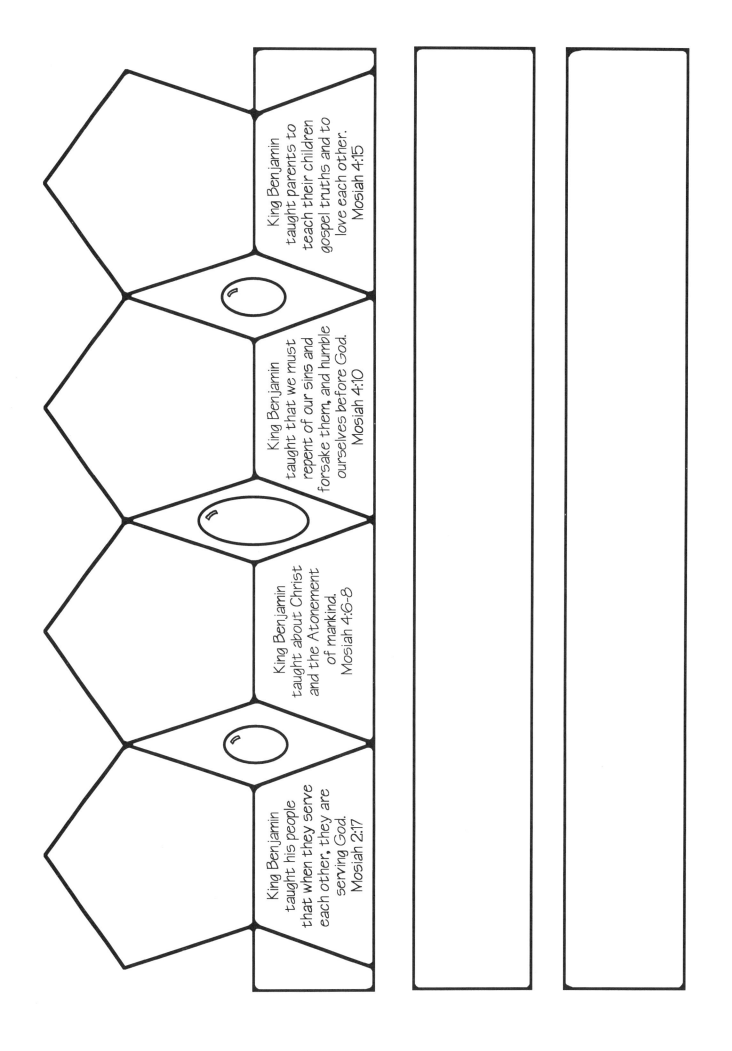

Joseph Smith's First Vision	The Baptism of Christ
The Ten Lepers	The Last Supper

The Word of Wisdom	The Law of Tithing
The Good Samaritan	Ammon, Missionary to the Lamanites

Noah and the Ark	Daniel in the Lion's Den
2,000 Stripling Warriors	The Brother of Jared

David and Goliath	The Atonement of Christ
The Holy Ghost	Modern-day Revelation

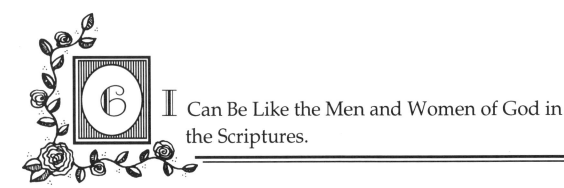

6 I Can Be Like the Men and Women of God in the Scriptures.

Preparation:

1. Copy and cut out the badges found on page 40—one badge for each child. Laminate badges, if desired.
2. Glue or tape a safety pin to the back of each badge.
3. Prayerfully choose five or six men and women from the scriptures and study their attributes and characteristics.
4. Gather a chalkboard, chalk, eraser, and permanent marker.

Lesson:

Across the top of the chalkboard, write the names of the men and women you have chosen from the scriptures. Discuss the story behind each individual and invite the children to contribute any information they have about those who are listed. During the discussion, list the notable qualities of each individual under their names. Discuss the importance of each quality and why we should strive to attain the same qualities. Allow the children time to choose a specific quality that they would like to develop in their life. Use the permanent marker to write the quality and the individual from the scriptures on each child's badge. Encourage the children to wear their badges often as a reminder of the quality they are working toward.

Additional Ideas:

• Copy the handout on page 41—one for each child. Make copies of the coat stripes on page 42. The number of copies needed will depend on how many children are in your Primary. Each child will need a total of four coat stripes, so each copy will serve three children. Cut the coat stripes apart. Gather scissors, crayons, and glue. Relate the story of Joseph and his coat of many colors by following the story parts on the picture of Joseph found on page 41 (see also Genesis 37 and 39-46). Give each child a picture of Joseph and four stripes. Have them color their pictures and stripes. Glue one edge of each stripe in place as indicated on the handout. Keep the other edge of the stripe unattached so that the stripes can be lifted one at a time to tell the story of Joseph. Encourage the children to relate the story of Joseph to their families and strive to live righteously as he did.

- At carnivals you will often see life-sized pictures of people where you can stand behind the figure and rest your chin on its shoulders so that it looks like your head is on someone else's body. Then you can have your picture taken. For your Primary class, if you know someone who is artistic, ask them to paint separate life-sized pictures of a righteous man and woman from the scriptures. If they paint the head, there is no need to paint the face since that area will be cut away to allow for the children's faces. If they don't want to paint the head, have them paint from the shoulders down and allow the children to rest their head on the shoulder of the painted figure. Attach the figures to some sort of frame or stand that allows a step stool to be placed in the back for the children to stand upon. Relate each story of the man and woman as found in the scriptures. Take a picture of each boy and girl as they place their face or head on the painted figures. Make copies of the frame on page 43—one for each child. When the film is developed, attach the picture to the center of the frame. Around the picture, write words that pertain to the person in the scriptures, such as "I can be obedient like Noah in the scriptures," or, "I can be courageous like Esther in the scriptures." Give each child their picture and encourage them to hang it where they can see it every day as a reminder to pattern their lives after the righteous people in the scriptures.

- Gather large pictures of your favorite men and women of God from the scriptures. Using sheets of paper large enough to cover each picture individually, cut each sheet of paper into 6-10 strips. For each group of paper strips, write clues about the identity of each individual—one clue for each strip of paper. Cover each picture by attaching the corresponding strips face-down to the picture with "Fun-tack." Display the covered pictures and have the children come forward one at a time and choose a strip. Remove the strip and read the clue. Have the child listen to the clue and look at the revealed part of the picture, and try to guess the identity of the person in the picture. Continue until all clues have been read, and all identities have been guessed. **Note:** You may prefer to reveal only one picture at a time so the children don't get the clues confused with each other.

- Invite bishopric-approved individuals from the ward to dress in costume and role play various men and women of God from the scriptures.

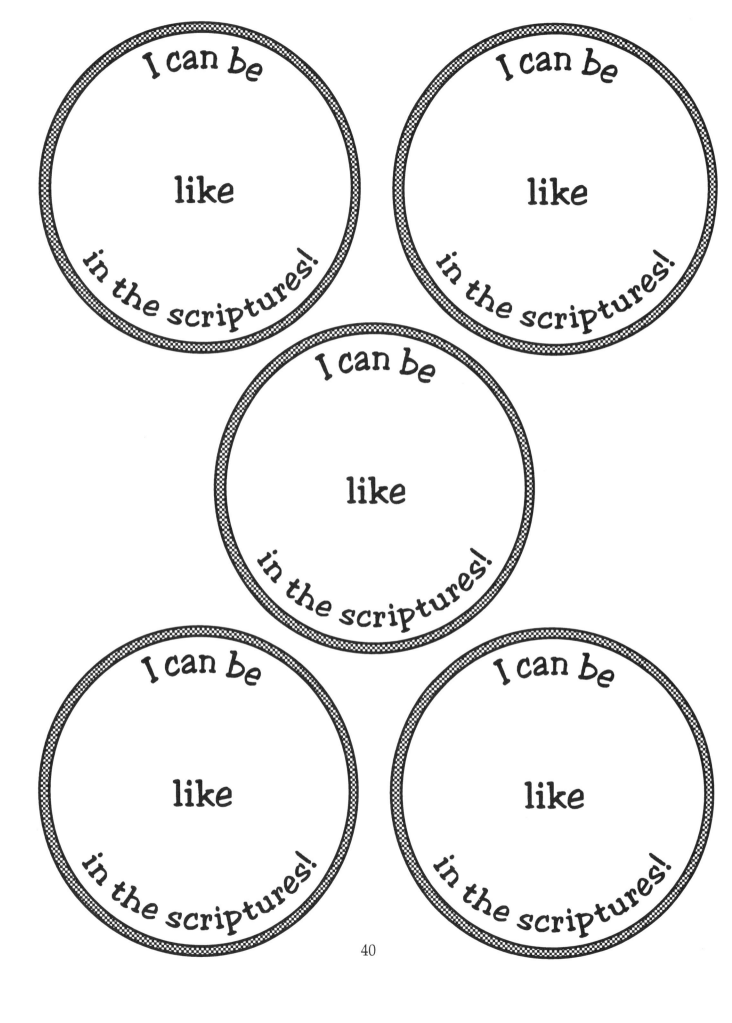

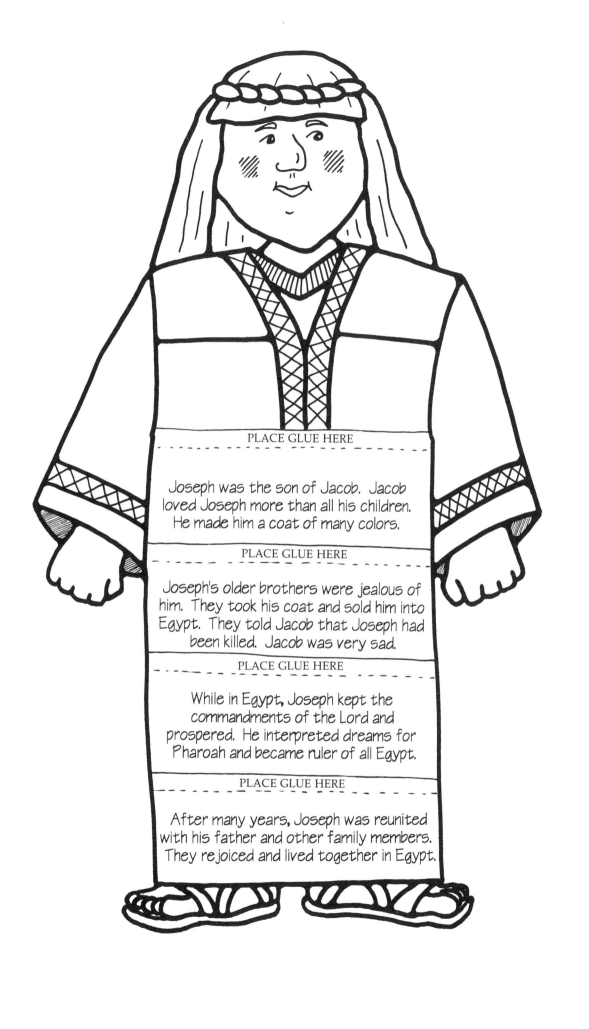

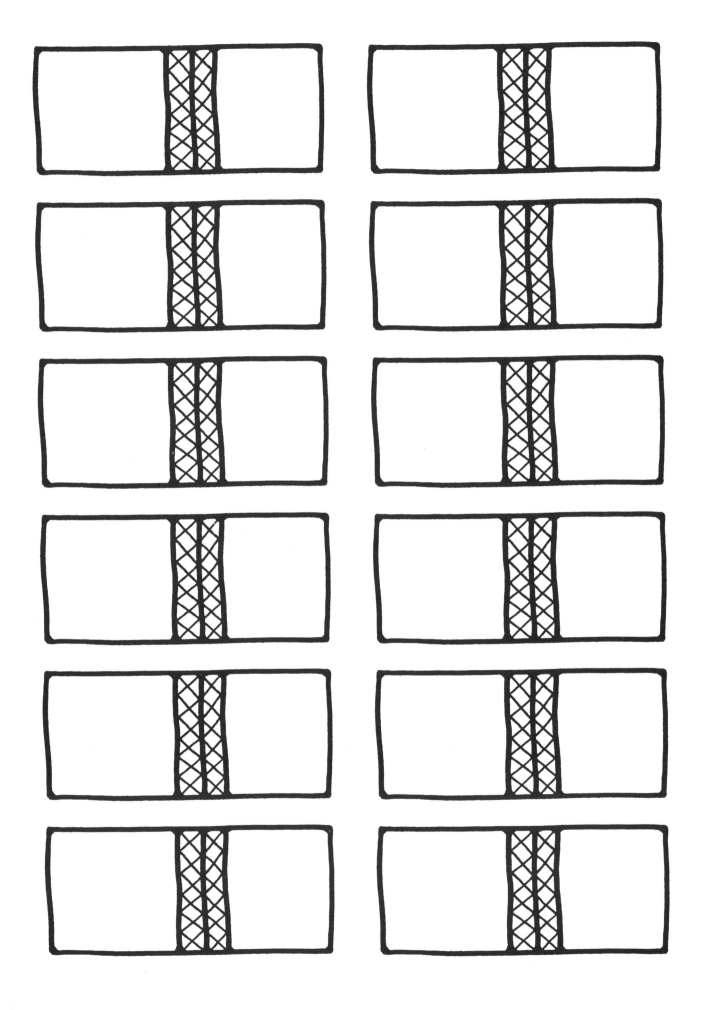

I Can Be

_____

like

_____

in the Scriptures!

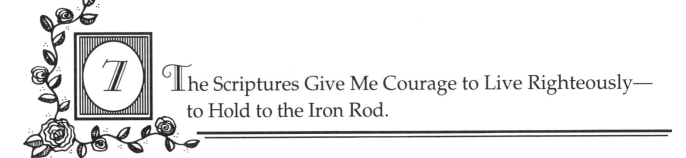

7. The Scriptures Give Me Courage to Live Righteously— to Hold to the Iron Rod.

Preparation:

1. Copy, color, and cut out pages 46 through 54.
2. Obtain "Fun-tack," and a display board.
3. Prayerfully study the scripture references given in the lesson below.

Lesson:

When the Lord gives a commandment, he always provides a way for his children to keep that commandment (see 1 Nephi 3:7). Display the pictures of Moses, Lehi, and Nephi as you tell their stories. Using the scripture references given on the pictures as a guide, begin with the story of Moses obeying the commandment to lead the children of Israel through the wilderness into the promised land. The Lord provided the way by parting the Red Sea, providing water from a rock, manna from heaven, and a brass serpent to heal their snake bites. The Lord also led them by day and was their light by night. Lehi was also commanded to lead his family through the wilderness toward the promised land. The Lord provided Lehi and his family with the Liahona, which by their faith and diligence pointed the way they should go, and also where they could find food to eat. The Lord allowed their meat to be sweet so that they could limit their use of fire. He was also their light in the wilderness and prepared the way for them. Nephi was commanded to build a ship that would carry them across the sea to the promised land. The Lord instructed him in the manner in which to build the ship. He showed Nephi where he could find ore to molten into tools. Nephi was able to make a bellows from animal skins and use fire to molten the ore. When Nephi's older brothers were angry with him and wanted to throw him into the depths of the sea, the power of the Lord was within Nephi, protecting him from his contentious brothers. These scripture stories and others help us to see that the Lord truly does provide a way for his children to keep his commandments. Encourage the children to have faith that the Lord will also provide a way for them to keep his commandments.

Additional Ideas:

- Invite bishopric-approved ward members to role play Lehi's dream of the iron rod found in 1 Nephi 8. Afterward, discuss the symbolism of the various parts of the dream. Encourage the children to be like the group that held to the rod and partook of the fruit. By following the commandments and enduring to the end, we will be blessed with eternal life.

- Divide the children into two groups. Give each group a piece of paper and a pencil. Invite one group to look up "COURAGE" in the Topical Guide. The other group can look up "RIGHTEOUSNESS." Give the groups time to find about 5-7 scriptures that give a good description of their word. Allow the groups time to report to the Primary the scriptures they have chosen.

- Divide the children into small groups. If possible, assign a Primary worker to assist each group. Give each group a story from the scriptures and where it is located. Have the groups take a few minutes to read over the story. When the time is up, let the groups take turns relating their story (in their own words) to the rest of Primary. Some possible stories of courage can be found in the *1998 Children's Sacrament Meeting Presentation and Sharing Time Outline.*

The Lord parted the Red Sea.

The Lord provided water from a rock.

The Lord sent manna from heaven.

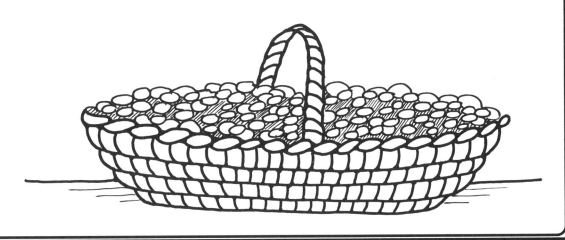

Those who beheld the serpent of brass were healed.

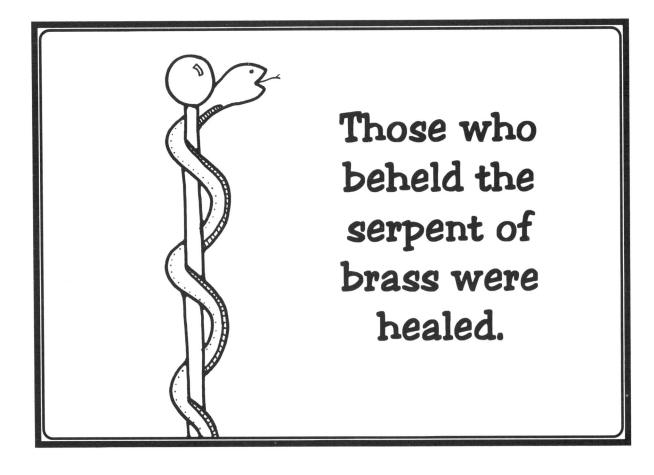

The Liahona guided their way.

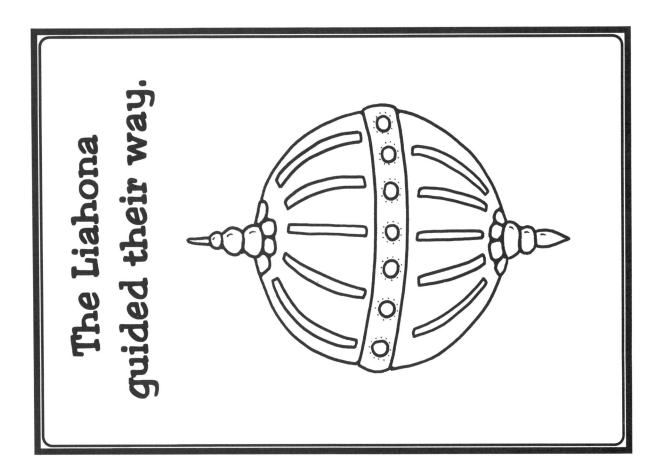

Fire was not needed to cook their food.

It was revealed to Lehi where they should hunt for food.

The Lord was their light in the wilderness.

The Lord instructed Nephi on how to build a ship.

Nephi melted ore by using a bellows to blow the fire.

Nephi made tools from molten ore.

The power of the Lord protected Nephi.

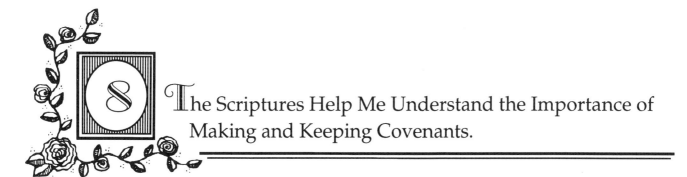

8. The Scriptures Help Me Understand the Importance of Making and Keeping Covenants.

Preparation:

1. Copy page 57 for the younger children. Copy the worksheet on page 58 for the older children.
2. Gather scissors, glue, and crayons for the younger children. Gather pencils for the older children.
3. Prayerfully study the covenants that are used as references on page 58.

Lesson:

What is a covenant? Bruce R. McConkie states, "In the gospel sense, a covenant is a binding and solemn compact, agreement, contract, or mutual promise between God and a single person or a group of chosen persons" (*Mormon Doctrine*, © Bookcraft, Inc., 1966, p. 166). In ancient times, God made many covenants with his children. For instance, he promised Noah never to flood the earth again and provided a rainbow as a token of his covenant. He promised Lehi that his seed would inherit the land of America forever. God continues to make covenants with his children today. To help the children learn about these covenants, pass out pencils and the worksheet found on page 58 to the older children. Encourage them to look up the references given so that they can fill in the blanks correctly. For the younger children, pass out the copies of page 57. Provide crayons, scissors, and glue. After the children have completed coloring the pictures, cut the paper along the heavy, solid line to the dot. Fold the paper to the back along the thin, solid lines. Fold the paper to the front on the dotted lines. When the booklet is folded, glue the backs of the pages together. There is no need for staples when the booklet is folded and glued properly. **Note:** Due to the fact that paper can shift slightly when photocopying, the folding and cutting lines may be off slightly. If this happens and you find that you need to trim the edges of the pages slightly after folding, be sure that you don't trim any of the folds. Encourage the children to refer to their booklets often to remind them of their covenants with the Lord.

Additional Ideas:

- Copy and color pages 59 through 61. Cut out the hearts on page 61. Trim page 59 and glue to page 60 as indicated. Gather "Fun-tack" and a display board. Place the house with the hearts surrounding it on the display board. Share the story of Joshua as found in Joshua 24:14-15, 24, and 31. Explain to the children that in this instance, "house" means family. Invite the children to come forward one at a time to choose a heart, locate and read the scripture reference, and discuss how it relates to serving the Lord. Continue until all the hearts have been placed on the house. Encourage the children to make their house (or family) one that serves the Lord daily.

- Prayerfully study the sacrament prayers found in Moroni 4:3 and 5:2—including the footnotes. Gather pictures that relate to the Atonement, such as Gethsemane, the crucifixion, the resurrection, the last supper, etc. Also gather pictures representing various commandments the Lord has given us. Finally, gather a picture of a child being baptized. Display the pictures. Help the children locate the sacrament prayers in their scriptures. Invite them to mark the prayers with a scripture marker. Discuss more fully the words and meaning of each prayer, referring to the various pictures throughout the discussion. Encourage the children to envision in their mind the pictures and their meanings each Sunday as the prayers are said.

Additional Resources:

- Relate the story of Noah as found in Genesis 9:8-17. Using the book, *Little Talks for Little People* (© 1994 Susan Luke, Covenant Communications, Inc.), copy pages 25 and 26 onto card stock—one set of copies for each child. Help the children make their own visual aids to retell the story by following the directions given on page 24 of the same book. You may want to provide a paraphrased copy of the story that can be glued to the back of the ark. The children can refer to this when retelling the story. **Note:** This project can take some time to color and cut out. To save time during sharing time, you may want to ask someone to help you cut out some of the pieces beforehand.

- Share with the children the Word of Wisdom as found in D&C 89. If we promise to obey the Word of Wisdom, Heavenly Father promises us health, strength, and hidden treasures of knowledge. Using the book, *Little Talks for Little People* (© 1994 Susan Luke, Covenant Communications, Inc.), copy pages 15 and 16 for each child. Allow time for the children to color the pictures. You may want to provide a paraphrased copy of the Word of Wisdom that can be glued to the back of the pictures. Encourage the children to go home and share with their families their knowledge of the Word of Wisdom.

The Lord promises to open the windows of heaven and pour out so many blessings that I won't be able to receive them all. 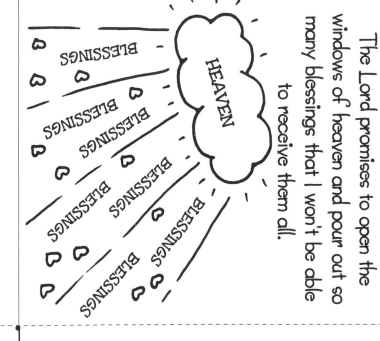	If I promise to pay one-tenth of everything I earn to the Lord...
If I promise to obey the commandments and keep the Sabbath day holy.... 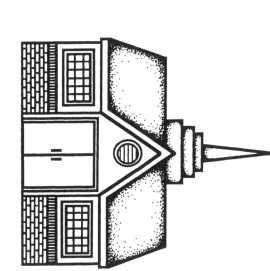	The Lord promises me health, wisdom, and great treasures of knowledge. 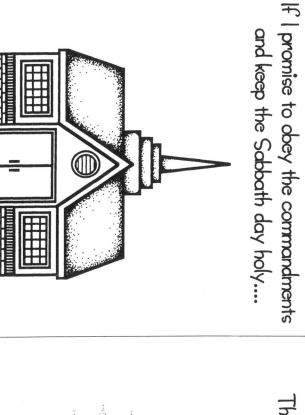
The Lord promises me eternal life with him. 	**A covenant is a two-way promise between the Lord and me.** If I promise to obey the Word of Wisdom by putting only healthy things into my body... 

Covenants

A covenant is a two-way promise between the Lord and an individual. Learn more about covenants by completing the scriptures below. You will need to look up each scripture reference given in order to fill in the blanks correctly.

D&C 136:4
"And this shall be our _____—that we will _____ in all the _____ of the _____."

Exodus 20:12
"_____ thy _____ and thy _____: that thy _____ may be long upon the _____ which the Lord thy God _____ thee."

D&C 89:18-20
"And all _____ who remember to keep and do these _____, walking in _____ to the _____, shall receive _____ in their navel and _____ to their bones; And shall find _____ and great treasures of _____, even hidden _____: And shall _____ and not be _____, and shall _____ and not _____."

Malachi 3:10
"Bring ye all the _____ into the _____, that there may be meat in mine _____, and prove me now _____, saith the Lord of _____, if I will not open you the _____ of heaven, and _____ you out a _____, that there shall not be _____ enough to receive it."

Mosiah 18:10-11
"Now I say unto you, if this be the _____ of your hearts, what have you _____ being _____ in the name of the Lord, as a _____ before him that ye have _____ into a _____ with him, that ye will _____ him and keep his _____, that he may pour out his _____ more abundantly upon you? And now when the _____ had heard these _____, they clapped their _____ for joy, and exclaimed: This is the _____ of our _____."

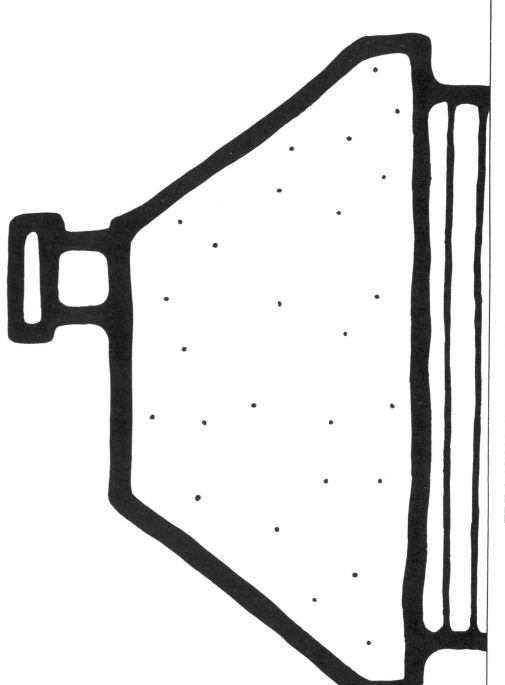

"Choose you this day whom ye will serve...but as for me and my house, we will serve the Lord." Joshua 24:15

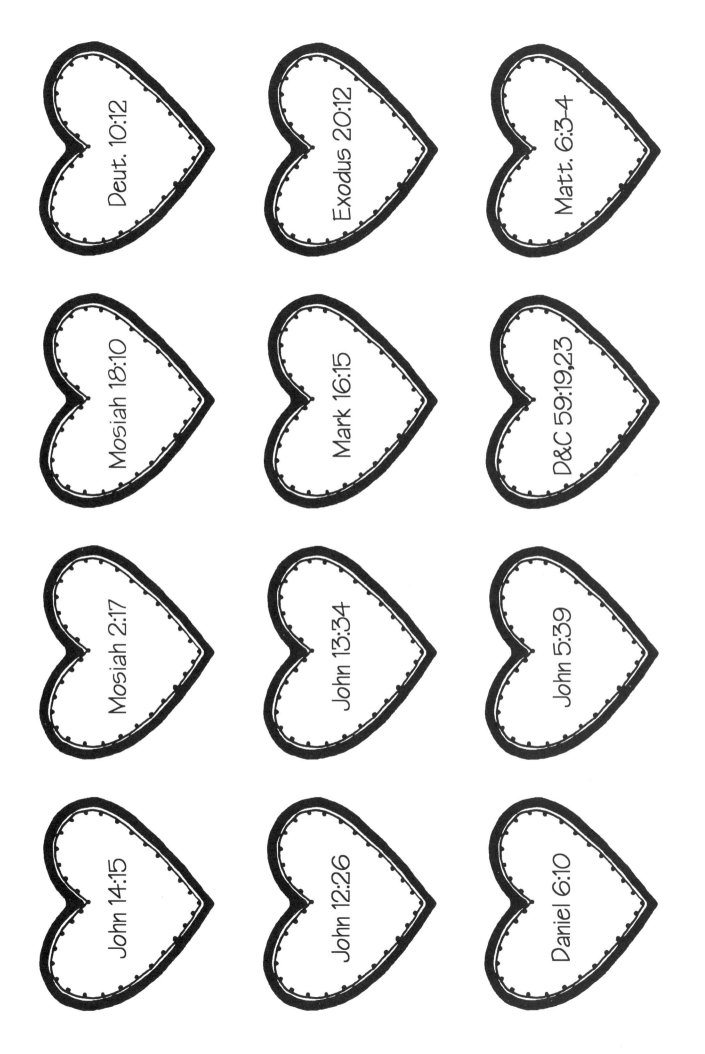

9 The Scriptures Teach Me That Heavenly Father Hears My Prayers.

Preparation:

1. Copy pages 65 and 66 onto white card stock. After cutting out the stones, turn them over and color around the outer edges with a yellow pencil, crayon, or highlighter so they appear to shine. You could also color around the finger of the Lord to make it shine.
2. Gather "Fun-tack," and a display board.
3. Prayerfully study the story of the Brother of Jared found in Ether 2:16-3:13.

Lesson:

Prior to sharing time, place the stones (with the numbers showing) on the display board. Share the story of the brother of Jared as found in Ether 2:16-3:13. Encourage the children to listen carefully so they can correctly answer the questions you will ask at the end of the story. When the story is finished, have the children come forward one at a time and choose a stone. Ask the questions below that correlate with the number on the stone. If the child answers correctly, touch the stone with the finger of the Lord, turn the stone over (so it shines), and place it back on the display board. Continue until all the stones have been touched by the Lord (questions answered correctly) and placed shining side up on the display board. Encourage the children to pray in faith as the brother of Jared did—believing that God will answer their prayers.

1. Who instructed the Jaredites to build barges? (the Lord)
2. Why were the Jaredites instructed to build barges? (to journey to the promised land)
3. How many barges did the Jaredites build? (8)
4. What did the Lord tell the brother of Jared to do to the barges in order to provide air to breathe? (make a hole at the top and at the bottom of the barges—unstopping them for air and stopping them when the water came in)
5. Besides the need for air in the barges, what other problem did the brother of Jared need the Lord's help in solving? (how to light the barges)
6. How many stones did the brother of Jared molten out of rock? (16)
7. Describe the stones that the brother of Jared did molten out of rock. ("white

and clear, even as transparent glass")
8. Where did the brother of Jared go to pray? (mount Shelem or a mount)
9. What did the brother of Jared want the Lord to do to the stones? (touch them so they would shine)
10. What did the brother of Jared see when the Lord touched the stones? (the finger of the Lord)
11. What did the brother of Jared do when he saw the finger of the Lord? (He fell to the earth in fear.)
12. Why was the brother of Jared scared when he saw the finger of the Lord? (He didn't realize the Lord had a body of flesh and bone and was afraid the Lord would smite him.)
13. What did the brother of Jared realize when he saw the finger of the Lord? (that the Lord had a body of flesh and bone)
14. In order to see the finger of the Lord, the brother of Jared had an exceeding amount of what? (faith)
15. Did the Lord show himself to the brother of Jared? (yes)
16. After the Lord showed many wonderful things unto the brother of Jared, what did the Lord tell him? ("Write these things and seal them up; and I will show them in mine own due time unto the children of men.")

Additional Ideas:

- Invite bishopric-approved members of the ward to share personal stories of when their prayers were answered—including prayers that were answered the way the Lord seemed to feel was best and not the way they had expected.

- Show the video segment "The First Vision" found on the video, *Moments from Church History* (53145). Conclude by bearing testimony that Heavenly Father hears and answers prayers just as he did for young Joseph Smith.

- Copy the strips found on page 67. Gather tape or a stapler. Explain to the children that prayer is our link to Heavenly Father. When we perform it the proper way, we can petition the Lord and receive answers to our prayers. Begin with the strip labeled "ME." Form a link from the strip and ask a child to come forward and hold it so the rest of the children can see it. Form a link from the strip labeled "HEAVENLY FATHER" and ask another child to come forward and hold it. Have the two children stand a small distance apart from each other. Invite other children to come forward one at a time and choose a strip. Read the scripture reference given on the strip and discuss why it is an important link in our prayer to Heavenly Father. Thread the strip through the link labeled "ME" and form it into another link. Continue reading, discussing, and linking each strip until the final strip is connected to "HEAVENLY FATHER" and the prayer is complete. Emphasize to the children that when we offer sincere prayers, we can be linked to Heavenly Father and receive his counsel.

- Play the part of the private detective as found in lesson three. Find evidence in the scriptures that Heavenly Father hears and answers our prayers.

Additional Resources:

- Share the talk "Daniel and the Lion's Den" found on pages 47-49 of *More Little Talks for Little People*. (© 1995 Susan Luke, Covenant Communications, Inc.) Make copies of the finger puppets that follow the talk—one set for each child. Allow the children to color and cut out their puppets. Place the puppets in an envelope and encourage the children to go home and retell the story to their family. **Note:** You will need to instruct the children on how to tape their puppets to fit their fingers when they get home. You may also want to include a reduced copy of the story in the envelope so the children can retell it correctly.

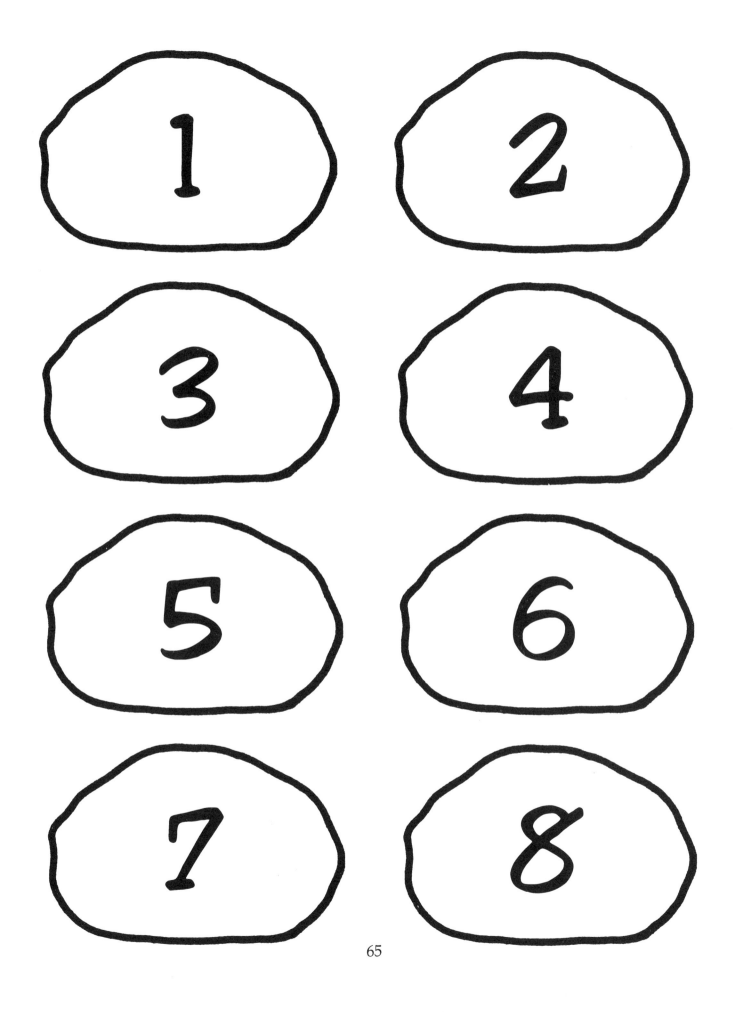

ME

Pray in secret/no vain repetitions
Matthew 6:6-7

Address Heavenly Father
Matthew 6:9

Thank the Lord
D&C 59:7

Ask the Lord in faith
James 1:5-6, 1 Nephi 15:11

Counsel with the Lord
Alma 37:37

Repent of your sins
Moses 5:8, JS-H 1:29

Pray always
D&C 19:38

Close in the name of Christ
Colossians 3:17

HEAVENLY FATHER

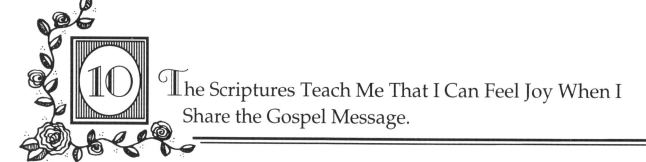

10 The Scriptures Teach Me That I Can Feel Joy When I Share the Gospel Message.

Preparation:

1. Make copies of page 70—one page will serve two children. Trim the papers to within 1/4" of the printed border.
2. Gather pens or pencils.
3. Invite the full-time missionaries to come to Primary so that you can present them with the testimonies of the children.

Lesson:

Share the missionary stories of the sons of Mosiah found in Alma 17-26. Be sure to emphasize the great joy they felt as they shared the gospel message with others. We can share the gospel with others in many ways—one of which is writing our testimony down on paper and placing it in a Book of Mormon before it is given away. Give each child a piece of paper and help children write their testimony of what joy the gospel brings to them. When finished, present the papers to the full-time elders to be placed in the copies of The Book of Mormon they give away.

Additional Ideas:

- Make copies of pages 71 and 72—one set for each child. Gather scissors, glue, and crayons. Prayerfully study the story of Jonah as found in Jonah 1-3. Share the story with the children. When finished, pass out the papers and allow the children to color and cut out Jonah and the whale along the outer, solid lines. (Don't cut the paper that has the dashed outline of the whale.) Glue around the outer edges of the whale (excluding the mouth) and fasten to the paper following the guidelines given. Encourage the children to share the story with their family—placing Jonah in the whale at the appropriate time.

- Invite bishopric-approved ward members or a family in the ward to role play the story of Ammon and King Lamoni (Alma 17-19; 26:10-16), or Alma and Amulek (Alma 8:8-9:34; 11:21-12:19.)

- Invite the full-time missionaries to share the joy they have experienced in sharing the gospel message with others. Other invited guests could be stake missionaries, the ward mission leader, or a ward family who has found joy in fellowshipping another family into the Church.

- Play the part of the private detective as found in lesson three. Find evidence in the scriptures that we can feel joy when we share the gospel message.

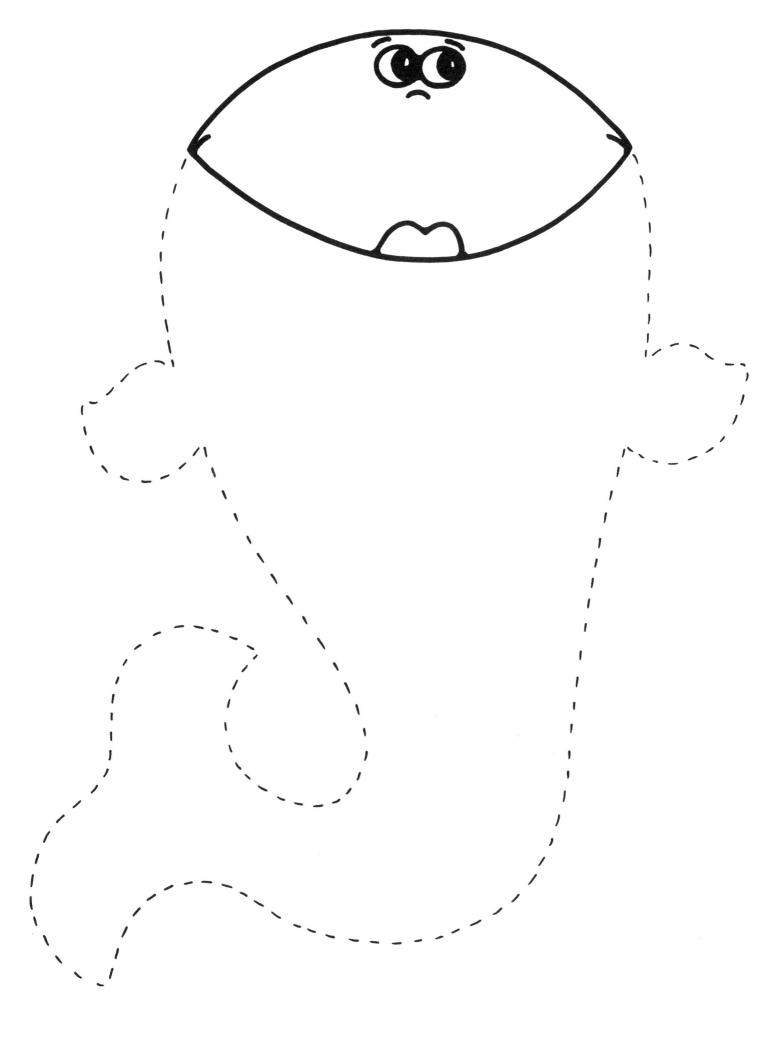

11 The Scriptures Help Me Feel Gratitude to Heavenly Father.

Preparation:

1. Copy and color pages 75 and 76. Cut out page 75.
2. Gather "Fun-tack" and a display board.
3. Prayerfully study the references given on the various flower parts.

Lesson:

President Lorenzo Snow once said, "It is the duty of every Latter-day Saint to cultivate a spirit of gratitude." When people want to grow a beautiful flower in their garden, they don't just throw a seed anywhere in the hope that it will take root and grow. Instead, they find the best possible place to plant the seed. A place with fertile soil and an abundance of sunshine. They water the seed daily and remove any weeds that might hamper its growth. They continue to nourish the seed until it grows into a beautiful flower—giving great pleasure to the gardener. As children of God, we are much like the flower in the garden. Heavenly Father has provided everything we need to grow. He nourishes and cares for us daily. We can show our gratitude for Heavenly Father by blossoming into a loving, Christ-like person. Place the picture of the soil and seed packet on the display board. Place the flower parts off to the side of the display board. Invite the children to come forward one at a time and choose a flower part. (It's best to start with the stem and leaves.) Have the children locate and read aloud the reference given on each part. Discuss how each reference helps us to cultivate a spirit of gratitude for Heavenly Father.

Additional Ideas:

- Look up the word "Gratitude" from the list of topics in the back of the *Children's Songbook*. Play "Name That Tune" with the songs listed.

- Give each child a "thank-you" card and have them express their thankfulness to Heavenly Father. Encourage them to take their cards home and place them in their journal or Book of Remembrance.

- Copy the scripture references on page 77—one copy for each child. Gather a small glass jar, tin can, or box for each child. Gather a variety of decorating supplies and allow time for the children to decorate their container. They could even label the container "An Attitude of Gratitude." Cut the strips apart and place them into each container. Encourage the children to develop an attitude of gratitude by reading the scripture references listed on the slips of paper with their family each day. Close by singing "I Thank Thee, Dear Father," *Children's Songbook*, p. 7. **Note:** You may use envelopes if small containers are not available.

- Obtain a long roll of white paper. Gather crayons, pencils, and felt pens. Prior to sharing time, write across the top (lengthwise) the words "Count Your Blessings." Begin sharing time by singing, "Count Your Blessings," hymn #241. Roll out the paper on the floor or across a couple of tables and let the children write or draw all the blessings they can think of given to them by Heavenly Father—prompting them as necessary. Display the mural in the Primary room when complete.

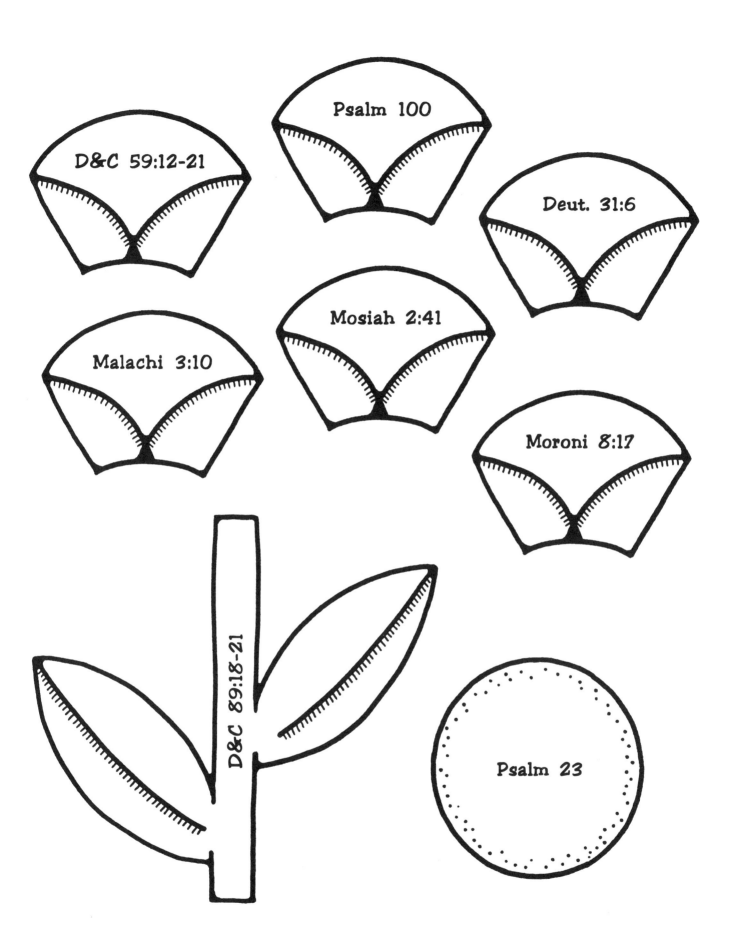

Alma 7:23

 Mosiah 2:19-22

 Alma 37:37

 1 Thessalonians 5:18

 D&C 46:31-33

 Colossians 3:15-17

 Ether 6:9

 Luke 17:11-16

 2 Nephi 9:52

 1 Corinthians 15:57

 Psalm 50:14-15

 Colossians 2:6-7

 Psalm 92:1-2

 Alma 34:37-38

 Psalm 100:1-5

 D&C 59:7

 Psalm 147:1

 D&C 78:19

 Philippians 4:6-7

 D&C 136:28

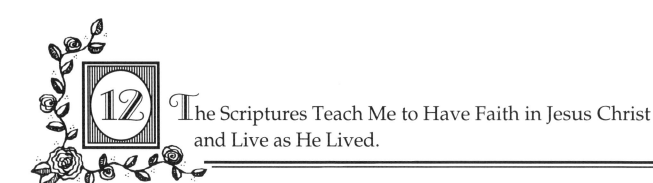

12. The Scriptures Teach Me to Have Faith in Jesus Christ and Live as He Lived.

Preparation:

1. Copy pages 80 and 81 for each child.
2. Gather crayons, scissors, and paper fasteners.

Lesson:

In Alma 37:38-47 we learn that Lehi and his family were led to the promised land with the help of the Liahona. Alma described the Liahona as a compass. As long as Lehi and his family were faithful, diligent, and heeded the direction of the Liahona, they progressed in their journey to the promised land. Alma also teaches us that just as the Liahona guided Lehi, the words of Christ will point us on a straight course to eternal bliss. The scriptures are the words of Christ. If we have faith and believe in Christ, he will lead us back to our Heavenly Father. Pass out the papers and allow time for the children to color. When finished, have the children cut along the outside edge of the circle. Carefully cut the opening as indicated on the paper. Place the circle to the back of the paper—lining up the black dots. Push a paper fastener through the dots. With the fastener secure, the circle should turn freely, showing the words of Christ through the opening. Encourage the children to follow the words of Christ so they can return to live with Heavenly Father.

Additional Ideas:

- Think of several things mentioned in the scriptures that Jesus did, such as heal the sick, walk on water, feed five thousand, etc. Write each item down on a separate slip of paper. Fold the slips in half and place them in a container. Invite the children to draw the slips from the container one at a time and act out what is written on the paper. The other children try to guess what it is that Jesus did. The child who guesses correctly takes the next turn.

- Copy pages 82 and 83 for each child. Gather scissors, glue, and felt pens or crayons. Have the children locate and read Alma 32:28-32 aloud. Alma taught us to experiment on the word of Christ. We are to give place in our heart for the word (seed) to be planted. If it is a good seed, it will grow within us—giving us increased understanding and blessings. Pass out the papers and allow time for the children to color their seeds and packets. Cut the packets along the outside lines and fold each flap to the back to create a packet. Glue the side flaps and bottom flap in place. Cut out the seeds. Each seed represents a principle that Jesus lived and taught. Discuss each seed as it is placed into the packet. Encourage the children to remove a seed each day, read the principle, and allow the "seed" to grow within them by following the principle that Jesus taught. As they do, they will come to know and appreciate the good seeds given to them by the Lord.

- Play the part of the private detective as found in lesson three. Find evidence in the scriptures of the way Christ lived so that we can follow his example.

After coloring page 80 and cutting away the opening as indicated, cut the circle below along the outside edge. Place the circle in back of the picture, lining up the black dots. Push a paper fastener through the dots. With the paper fastener secure, turn the wheel to reveal through the opening the words of Christ found in the scriptures.

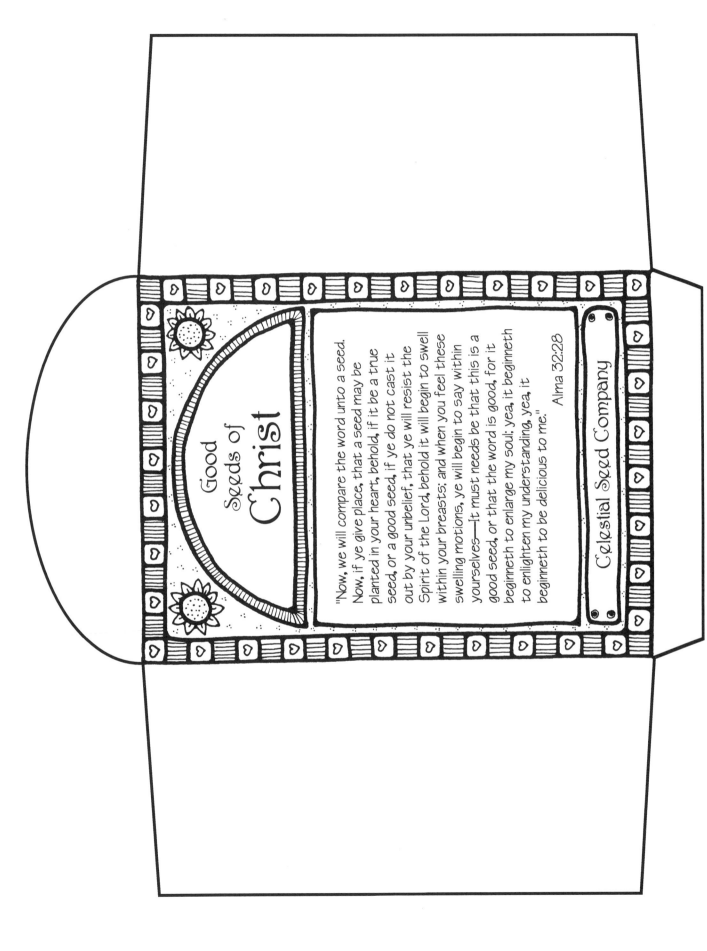

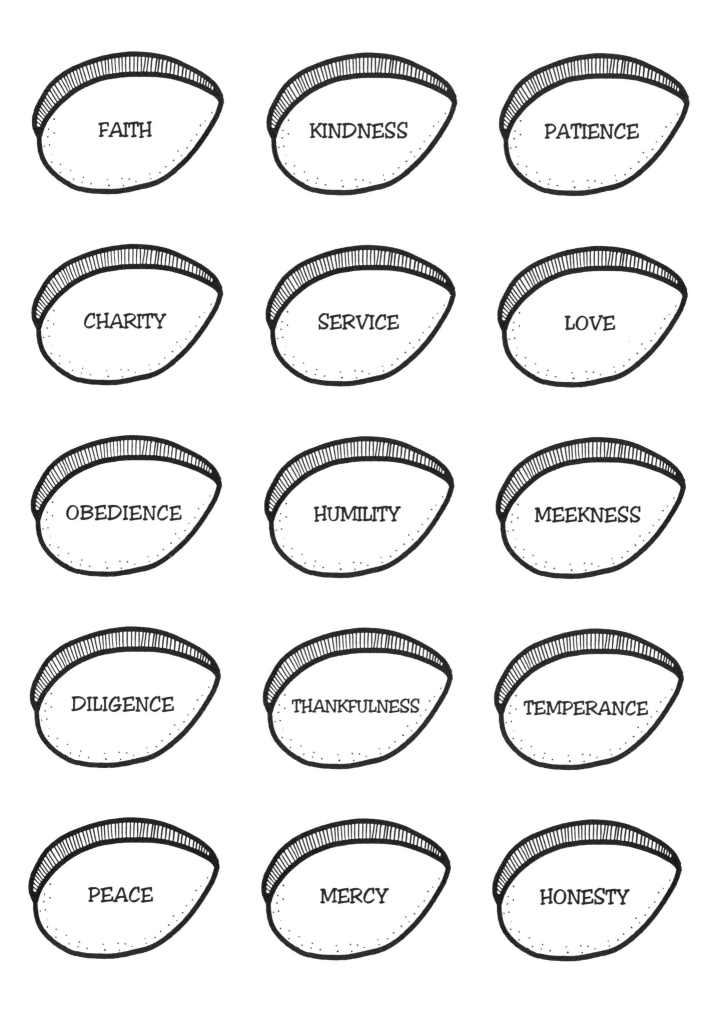

Monthly Scriptures

It is suggested in the *1998 Children's Sacrament Meeting Presentation and Sharing Time Outline* that children memorize the italicized scripture that supplements each month's theme. To help children memorize each scripture, copy pages 85-87 onto card stock—one set for each child. Cut the scripture cards apart and punch a hole in the corner of each card as indicated by the circle. Fasten each set of cards with a metal ring or ribbon. Give each child a set of cards and encourage them to memorize each scripture. **Note:** You may want to give the children one card each month instead of the whole set at once.

Memorization Tips

- Read the same scripture several times each day until it becomes familiar. Try closing your eyes and reciting the scripture from memory—peeking only when necessary.

- After reading through a scripture a few times to become familiar with it, write the first letter of each word on a piece of paper. Try to recite the scripture by using only the first letters as a prompt.

- As you become familiar with a scripture, cover a few key words. Recite the scripture. Continue covering and reciting until all the words are covered and you are reciting from memory.

- Sing the words of a scripture to a familiar tune—maybe a Primary song!

"And when ye shall receive these things, I would exhort you that ye would ask God, the Eternal Father, in the name of Christ, if these things are not true; and if ye shall ask with a sincere heart, with real intent, having faith in Christ, he will manifest the truth of it unto you, by the power of the Holy Ghost. And by the power of the Holy Ghost ye may know the truth of all things."   Moroni 10:4-5

2

"I am the way, the truth, and the life: no man cometh unto the Father, but by me."   John 14:6

4

"The Lord God will do nothing, but he revealeth his secret unto his servants the Prophets."   Amos 3:7

1

"And this is life eternal, that they might know thee the only true God, and Jesus Christ, whom thou has sent."   John 17:3

3

"I did liken all scriptures unto us, that it might be for our profit and learning." 1 Nephi 19:23

5

"Trust in the Lord with all thine heart; and lean not unto thine own understanding. In all thy ways acknowledge him, and he shall direct thy paths." Proverbs 3:5-6

6

"I will go and do the things which the Lord hath commanded, for I know that the Lord giveth no commandments unto the children of men, save he shall prepare a way for them that they may accomplish the thing which he commandeth them." 1 Nephi 3:7

7

"Ye have entered into a covenant with him, that ye will serve him and keep his commandments, that he may pour out his Spirit more abundantly upon you." Mosiah 18:10

8

"For I am not ashamed of the gospel of Christ: for it is the power of God unto salvation to every one that believeth." — Romans 1:16

10

"Yea, come unto Christ and be perfected in him." — Moroni 10:32

12

"If any of you lack wisdom, let him ask of God, that giveth to all men liberally, and upbraideth not; and it shall be given him." — James 1:5

9

"Thou shalt thank the Lord thy God in all things." — D&C 59:7

11

OTHER BOOKS BY SUSAN LUKE

EXPERIMENTS UPON THE WORD

There's nothing like a good object lesson—something you can see, feel, taste, or experience—to help you make a point. And if you've ever faced a captive audience in a church class or during family home evening, you know that a great object lesson can often mean the difference between a ho-hum endurance session and an aha! learning experience.

Popular author Susan Luke takes dozens of simple scientific experiments and ingeniously applies them to gospel principles. The result is an exceptional book of fun, easy, and exciting object lessons that will bring gospel concepts instantly to life for students of any age. They're perfect for:

- Primary classes and Sharing Time
- Sunday School
- Young Women/Priesthood/Relief Society
- Family Home Evening

POSITIVELY PRIMARY

A must for every Primary leader! In these pages you'll find a wealth of simple, clever, workable ideas that you can use to make your Primary meetings more colorful, efficient, fun, and inviting. From ribbons and certificates for special recognition, to lively classroom and seating markers, to "Wow! What a Class!" posters, to Primary newsletters, journals, and "Clutter Control" badges, you'll have the tools you need to make even the most ordinary Primary something extraordinary!

If you've always dreamed of having a wonderful Primary, this book will positively help you reach your goal!

FANTASTIC FAMILY NIGHTS!

Here's a book that has everything you need to quickly plan effective, fun, creative family nights. Now you can make your family home evenings a time all the kids look forward to . . . no more moping around or dragging their feet.

This book includes ideas for games, activities, lessons, charts, and visual aids. You will find a wealth of resources that will help you fulfill your responsibility to your family without having to spend undue amounts of time in preparation.

Be a more effective teacher, have more fun with your family, and feel the satisfaction of following the important counsel to gather your family together for fantastic family nights!

AWESOME FAMILY NIGHTS

Here's help to make family home evening the week's biggest attraction! Whether you're looking for thought-provoking gospel themes, exciting activities to promote family unity, fun games that teach gospel principles, or handy hints for family involvement, you'll find them in this volume of outstanding family night ideas!

Thirteen brand-new lessons teach children important gospel principles in fun, interesting ways; and the book also includes excellent ideas for a variety of games, activities, charts, visual aids, and even refreshments.

With this book in hand, you can look forward to week after week of *Awesome Family Nights!*

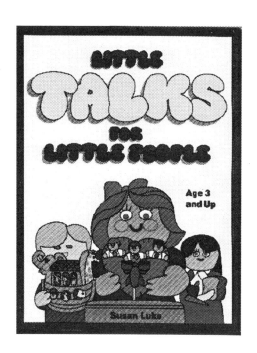

LITTLE TALKS FOR LITTLE PEOPLE

Here's everything you need to help your child give a fun, meaningful talk—complete with visual aids!

Includes text and visual aids for a dozen brief talks that children can learn quickly and enjoy presenting. Short sentences make them excellent for very young children. Simple, thorough instructions show a child exactly how to prepare the visual aids and give the presentations.

So simple that older children can easily help a younger one to prepare and present them. Your family will use, re-use, and enjoy them until all the "Little People" have become "Big People"!

MORE LITTLE TALKS FOR LITTLE PEOPLE

A second volume of fun, easy-to-prepare talks for the "little people" in your life. Whether your child is a natural-born speaker or a bit on the shy side, he or she will love putting together these talks and presenting them at Primary, home evening, and other family get-togethers.

This volume provides text and visual aids for a baker's dozen brief talks that children can learn quickly and enjoy presenting. Subjects include "My Testimony," "Daniel and the Lion's Den," "Prayer," "Songs of the Heart," "Tithing," "The True Meaning of Christmas," and seven more. Both the "big people" and the "little people" in your family will enjoy them for years to come!

SUPER SUNDAYS!

Games, puzzles, service projects, music, and more are included in this treasure trove of Sabbath activities. From creating an Articles of Faith mobile, to performing a puppet show using scripture characters, to playing Book of Mormon Dominoes or Gospel Bingo, these activities are fun, interesting, varied, simple to do, and help teach important gospel principles. Best of all, they can be done reverently in keeping with the spirit of the Sabbath.

Dozens of projects that your family can enjoy and repeat year after year. Don't let another Sunday go by without having this book in your home!